What Do You Live For?

What Do You Live For?

ANSWERS TO THE UNAPPROACHABLE QUESTIONS

MAYA HUANG

Foreword

500 people were asked one question:
What do you live for?

Many could not answer. But for those who could, the very
core essence of their lives is recorded on the following pages.

Contents

PART ONE

For Others

"My family. I know it's a cliche but to see my son's smiling face, feel my daughter kicking inside me, and being in my husband's warm arms are my reasons for living. Everything I do is for them, and I hope that everyone can experience this kind of love in their life."

Two

"I live for my niece. Nothing more. I've been suicidal for a while now, but her being born into this world makes me stay. I want to see her grow."

Three

"Honestly, I live to make other people smile. Charlie Chaplin is a huge inspiration to me in that sense. If I can make just one person's day by giving them a few laughs, I consider that to be a successful day."

Four

"I live for my cat and my dog. I love waking up every morning and seeing them snuggled up with me and my boyfriend on the bed. I love coming home and being greeted by them at the door, anxiously waiting for my love and affection. Being with them is the highlight of my day and I know they love me very much. They both came from bad homes, and I wake up every day and make sure they have the best possible home with me."

Five

"I have to feed my cat."

Six

"My dad. I tried to kill myself once and when I woke up in the hospital, he was crying and told me how much it would break his heart if I killed myself. I haven't attempted since."

Seven

"My daughter. She's what keeps me out of trouble and keeps me going from day to day."

Eight

"My family. My mom has an incurable disease, my brother has a mood disorder, and my dad confides in me. So, I figure it would be selfish of me to contemplate anything other than continuing to live on."

Nine

"I'm living for my best friend, whom I've never met. She's in Ukraine, and one day we're gonna meet."

Ten

"I live because I don't want to let my parents down. When they die, I'm going to dedicate my life to drugs."

Eleven

"Up until 55 days ago, I got up for one thing alone: to cop
heroin and shoot that shit. That part of my life lasted the
better part of a decade. Today, I have become aware of things
beyond myself, beyond my ego. I lived so selfishly for so long
that I'm having a tough time getting outside myself, but it's
beginning to happen. When I wake up, I ask the universe what
I might do to help someone else rather than myself. Strangely,
I still feed my ego by doing these things, but it is a much less
fleeting way to do so. To be honest, I live to see other people
thrive. It's the only thing keeping me from slipping back into
that empty, hedonistic lifestyle I suffered through for the last
ten years."

Twelve

"I have the burning desire to do something in the world that will improve it for the people that come after me. Especially my kids."

Thirteen

"My fiancé and our, as of now, theoretical children. Louis CK said it best, 'If you're single, your life has no consequence on the Earth'. Even if you're helping people aggressively, which you're fuckin' not, nobody gives a shit what happens to you. You can die and it actually doesn't matter."

Fourteen

"I think my answer would change quite often. But my birthday is this month. My two-year-old has decided to wish me a happy birthday every night this month when I tuck him in. That's what I'm currently living for."

Fifteen

"In all honesty, I don't know why I get out of bed every day. Most of my time is filled in the service of others. I'm told I'm a self-sacrificing, genuine people pleaser. I can't say that I have many activities that I do for myself. I'm not even sure I have any. I go to work every day for a paycheck but most of my money goes to other people. Either as gifts, groceries, or even just time away to have fun. It pleases me to know that through my hard work, I can make a difference in someone's life. When shit happens and it seems too much, I like to be there. The end results are better than could ever be expected. The smiles and thank you's I get make me feel so happy that anything I had to give be it money, time, or even a small gesture of kindness is what I live for. Does that seem weird?"

Sixteen

"I live for my 2 very young kids. I'm all they have left."

Seventeen

"I live to make people happy. There's nothing more satisfying than treating and helping out anyone and everyone I can."

Eighteen

"To make someone else's day better. Think of a time when someone did that for you and how much it meant. Now try to do that for another person in any way you can at least once a day. Even if it's just holding a door, it doesn't take too much to make someone else feel better."

Nineteen

"I live for my family. I have a one-year-old and a wonderful fiancé. I'm getting married this coming January. I've learned that you don't need money or material things to make you happy. So yeah, life is good."

Twenty

"Others. Seems sad, but I'm only really ever happy when people around me are happy, or if I'm making them happy. I help whenever I can and do anything I'm physically able to, to make their life easier."

Twenty-One

"Making my three-year-old enjoy life and fishing."

Twenty-Two

"Five months ago, I wouldn't have been able to give you a
direct answer. Sure, I have a wonderful wife, and a loving
family, but really to say, 'what do I live for?', no way. Now my
son, about 4 months old, gives me this feeling: I WANT to live
for him! I want to see him grow up, help him up if he falls, and
guide him through his life as my father did for me. I hope I am
able to teach him to be a good human being in this sometimes
awful world."

Twenty-Three

"For the possibility that I might one day have a little boy or girl
to whom I can show the world."

Twenty-Four

"Without a doubt, for my little brothers. We grew up super poor and I was the first one in the family to go to college. I want my brothers to have a quality education like I did, even if it means me paying the money for it."

Twenty-Five

"One day I want to look after my dad like he has my whole life.
That's my life aim."

Twenty-Six

"I guess the only reason I live is for my family. My dad works out of state most of the time and my mom goes to school. So it just leaves me with 4 other younger disabled kids. There are five of us and we all have autism that ranges in severity. I basically run a hospital at my house. Constant medication schedules and attention. Not to mention my school and education. My parents decided to homeschool me so I can stay at home 24/7. They say I'm "blessed" for having mild autism and being able to help out. They pretty much ripped me away from my social life and planned out my life for education and hard work. I expressed my desire to become an animator, but my parents won't stand for it seeing as it doesn't pay well. They think that I should get a job that supports the family. After a couple of years of this, I guess I have grown into it. My main goal in life is to get a good job and help my siblings and parents when they get old. And if that means giving up my dream, I have to do it. It does sound bad, but I would rather suffer than have to see my siblings live a life where people don't accept them."

Twenty-Seven

"To make sure no guys hit on my little sisters."

Twenty-Eight

"My nieces. It started with the first one. As soon as she was born, I knew I wanted to see her grow and always be there to help her."

Twenty-Nine

"Bettering my life for my children... which, to be honest, is sort of at rock bottom now. Finding someone after being cheated on and divorced is difficult, but I know why I'm powering through it."

Thirty

"My kids! I had a bad childhood. So, I want them to be healthy
and happy."

Thirty-One

"I'm a physician and biologist. I like my profession, I like getting better at it, and I like helping other people get better at it. Helping my patients gives satisfaction—when you see people doing better."

"Ultimately, my daughter. She was unplanned and I wasn't prepared, so I'm playing catch-up. Trying to find a good job, trying to find a better place to live, and trying to be a positive role model for her. I am always worried that I'm messing something up, but I am always trying to do what I think is right for her. I want her to have a better life than I did, and I want her to enter the adult world as a strong, beautiful woman who knows what she wants and how to get it. I don't want her to flounder in poverty like I have. She is now, but I am working hard to get us out of poverty, off government and parental assistance, and building a better future for her."

Thirty-Three

"I'm a single dad, so my son. This sounds like a simple cop-out type answer but really, it's a bit more than this. You see, I'm not a very emotional person. I don't frequently get sad nor happy. Imagine one's emotions as a rock. Someone emotional is a tiny round rock easily pushed one way or the other. Mine is a heaping big somewhat roundish boulder, sitting in a depression–of course, physical, not emotional.

But then there's my son. He's four years old. He's nothing but a bundle of positive energy. He is sweet, he shares on his own accord, and is, objectively speaking, the best child I've known. He doesn't take stupid risks, and nor has he ever...he's jumped off the couch once and before doing it he put a bundled-up blanket where he was jumping. He's also done what no one else has–not my parents, my family, not my ex-wife. His presence and even the thought of him cause what I can only describe as a current of happiness. Slow, firm, inexorable joy pushes at me. A little guy can move a big boulder."

PART TWO

For Future

Thirty-Four

"Curiosity for what the next moments of my life hold.
Curiosity is the reason to live."

Thirty-Five

"The world. The future. If I had the option for immortality, I would probably take it. The way the world has evolved and how we as a species have progressed through the ages fascinates me. I would love to see what the world is going to be like in 300 years. I enjoy reading all the amazing creations and new ideas people come up with every day."

Thirty-Six

"My potential. I know that I have the potential to be great. I know that eventually, I will have the discipline to harness it, but until then I'm just a time bomb."

Thirty-Seven

"To feel and see all things new. For the last three years, I've lived on the cheapest kind of bread and peanut butter, I have also worked at some shitty festivals selling food for 15h/day for 3 days straight, and just now work some hours at a printing industry... All so I can afford to go to Australia someday. That has been my goal for the last 4 years. My social life has been affected since I don't buy alcohol or go to parties, I also lost 11 lbs. of weight during my bread diet. But slowly I gained the money I needed for my trip, and soon I'll be off. Just one driver's license away."

Thirty-Eight

"To see where my journey goes. I like not knowing what the hell might happen to me next."

Thirty-Nine

"I was going to say that I get up in the morning because there is no other option. But I think, in reality, I get up because of the hope that things will get better. If I ever lose hope, I might stop getting up."

Forty

"To see what happens when I grow up. Kind of like reading a good book, there are so many options and you just sort of sit there and see where it brings you."

Forty-One

"The promise that something interesting will happen in the future. The promise that I can do something interesting or come up with something that amazes even me. Life is more fun like that."

Forty-Two

"I linger on in the vague hope that someday something will occur that will change my unfulfilling life forever. Something that will change my outlook and give me the motivation to find my place in this world. Because for 20 or so years I have felt powerless, unable to alter the course of my life in any meaningful way. Even the small things slip from my grasp."

Forty-Three

"As a teenager, I live for the huge potential that my future holds and for the hope that when I finally get to take these fucking training wheels off of my life, I won't just fall over."

Forty-Four

"I'm not sure what I will live for now, but I'm pumped for the future. I want to have a child and raise him the same way my father raised me. All that's left is to figure out who I am, finish college, and get a girlfriend."

Forty-Five

"Honestly, my main motivation for living is to see how we progress as a species; what we discover, what we accomplish. What is inevitably churned out by the curious mind is an inconceivable thought, and I want to be here to witness it."

Forty-Six

"Mostly I'm just really excited about what tomorrow might bring. Generally speaking, my life is pretty mundane. I go to class, hang out with friends, and play video games, but I'm really looking forward to the crazy stuff people are working on every day. I know at some point I'll get to see mankind land on Mars, advances in nanotechnology, and people with cybernetic limbs, and every day that passes brings me closer to witnessing this."

Forty-Seven

"I want to see the first man land on Mars. I want to see diseases cured, and I want to be at the forefront of the civil rights movement for androids–if that becomes a thing in my lifetime, anyhow. There are a lot of scientific discoveries I want to see that might not even be possible– quantum-entanglement facilitated FTL transport for complex structures first and foremost among them. If I could die knowing humanity could colonize the furthest reaches of the galaxy, I would die very happy. I live because life is really damn entertaining and interesting. More interesting than non-existence, to be sure."

PART THREE

For Love

Forty-Eight

"Love! I live for the love I feel, the love I give, the love of the future..."

Forty-Nine

"As cliché as it sounds, I live for love. I do not remember a time when I didn't like someone. It's what I find most important in our lives, to find the right person to love. And to love oneself. Also, happiness and harmony. I was probably a carebear in my past life. Maybe this is some kind of psychological thing, and it stems from issues, but I do not see any other worthwhile purpose for myself."

Fifty

"I drag myself to work every morning so I will be able to meet my boyfriend who lives 1000 miles away from me. I need about $1000 to get there, but it will be worth it in the end."

Fifty-One

"My wife. Always."

Fifty-Two

"For love. Easily. Just moved 3,000 miles to be with a girl I'd known less than a year. Haven't regretted it even a little bit at all. She's a keeper."

Fifty-Three

"For the girl I love."

Fifty-Four

"I love my wife and I want to see her have the best life I can possibly give her. Other than that, I'm cool with dying."

Fifty-Five

"I live for love. I felt it for the first time this summer. If you asked me this question before mid-July, I would have unequivocally answered with what I've lived by for as long as I can remember: career. Career, success, money, fame, legacy, impact. That's why I've been living a mundane day-to-day routine for over a decade. I woke up at 6 am every day for school, extracurriculars, and competitions, and I would finish my work at 2 am. I had huge groups of friends, and we were "close," but I was only capable of seeing them as means to various ends. In my mind, they weren't true friends. They were connections. I never took breaks, I never let myself rest, and I promised I would keep putting myself through this until I had succeeded. I thought I was happy. I thought I was content living this life, as the vague promise of delayed gratification pushed me through repetitive cycles of psychological torture every single day. I thought that my pride in my unyielding self-discipline was enough to keep me satisfied. On the inside, I knew I was wrong. I could feel myself slipping very gradually. But I continued–it was all I knew how to do. This summer, however, was jarring. I met someone who disrupted the way I viewed the world entirely. Unfortunately, I may never see him again. It is incredibly ill-fated that our paths were only destined to cross once. But I will never forget him. I live for the possibility of finding love again."

PART FOUR

For Me

Fifty-Six

"This might not be popular, but I live for me. Everything I do is for me. I'm trying to have the best experience that life could offer and make my life as enjoyable as I can. I think we all just do stuff for our own happiness. We're all selfish bastards."

Fifty-Seven

"Myself. I think that depending on others or material things for happiness is a recipe for disaster. Most things in life are temporary, bar yourself."

Fifty-Eight

"Masturbation. It is everything to me."

Fifty-Nine

"I'm starting to learn to live for myself and to make myself a better person in all aspects: physically, mentally, emotionally. I used to think I just wanted a relationship and a wonderful girlfriend/wife so that we could help keep each other afloat on whatever our path through life is. I've recently learned that it isn't what I need. I wish I knew how to take on life. It's not easy. I just wake up, pay the bills, and look toward my next big experience. Even though I've learned that love isn't the only important part of my life, I still managed to find someone who seems perfect for me. We've been together for almost a year now, though she moved away for grad school. I just got back from seeing her over the weekend. I've also learned that I shouldn't think of romantic lust as trust. I've had that throw me off too many times before. It was hard to differentiate between the two. I'm learning to trust her with myself, and she's been accepting every step of the way. It's one of the most amazing feelings.

But, aside from that- I'm getting fit. I'm getting healthy. I've been weightlifting and it feels amazing after a good workout.

I'm also bad at post-workout stretching, so I'm going to start doing Yoga. I'm stoked. I'm stoked about being awesome. I'm stoked about being a better me. I'm looking forward to whatever challenges await me. I want to dive head-on into everything. I just wonder if time will allow it..."

Sixty

"I live for the thrill of it all. I always ask myself, "how am I going to make today better than yesterday?" I am an entrepreneur and am always looking for ways to improve my situation financially, emotionally, and physically. After being in a deep depression for over a year this feeling is fantastic. I'm financially on something big and am on pace to net my first million by 2016."

Sixty-One

"I'm trying to compile skills and other stuff I can add to my list of things I can do. For example, I speak three languages and I can make digital music. I can also do useless stuff like juggling, armpit farting, flapping my ears, and crossing my eyes. An eclectic life purpose, but that's what I live for."

Sixty-Two

"To prove that I'm good at something."

Sixty-Three

"I live for me. I live for interaction with someone because it makes me feel better. Living for other people's needs and wants doesn't make you happy. Only fulfilling your desires makes you happy."

Sixty-Four

"I don't live for anything in particular. The only purpose in life is the purpose I give it... But all in all, I live for my happiness. Love, success, and satisfaction are all forms of happiness in one way or the other."

Sixty-Five

"I get to get up every day, laugh at jokes from my friends, smile at a cute girl I pass on the street and watch her blush, I get to feel a rush when I make someone proud, learn something I never knew before, teach other people my knowledge, have pride in knowing someone has represented me incredibly well, blush after I get smiled at from a cute girl who passes on me on the street, make my friends laugh. I try to reciprocate every positive emotion someone gives me onto someone else. It started out as a lie, I wasn't necessarily happy to see someone, but just saying the words to someone can make it true for them. Each person I interacted with became happy to see me and as a result, I became happy to see them.

I am incredibly lucky to be able to feel the way I do today about everything, and it wasn't always so easy to feel genuinely happy all the time. I am grateful for everyone in my life who has made me who I am today, whether that be the bully in 5th grade who picked on me, and caused me to stand up for someone being picked on, the girl I loved more than anything who cheated on me and broke my heart, helping me to learn she wasn't my greatest love and when I find her, it's going to be even better than I thought it could ever be, for every moment good or bad that has led me here to today, I couldn't have become this happy without every moment in my life."

PART FIVE

For Passion

Sixty-Six

"Music! Composing, recording, and performing songs with my instruments. Without this creative outlet, life would be even more meaningless than it already is."

Sixty-Seven

"I live to someday create a work of art that will last long after
I'm gone."

Sixty-Eight

"I just had an epiphany and suddenly wanted to go traveling. I changed everything about my life so I could save money. Cheaper accommodations, walking to work, quitting smoking, eating super cheap, no booze. I saved £10000 in just over a year and then I quit my job, packed my bags, and went. I set myself one rule; overground only, no planes. I have no regrets."

Sixty-Nine

"Mathematics. At the end of every day, I know a little more than I did that morning, and one of these days that knowledge will be uniquely mine - a tiny idea that will, with my name attached, be added to the unfathomably vast collection of already existing human knowledge. But before I share it, I will hold on to it for at least a day. No matter how desperately I want to share it with someone else, I will resist the temptation for 24 hours. I will use this time to quietly bask in the fact that I alone have proof of a new theorem, or an answer to a problem that no one else has solved. For a day, I will know something no one else does. I live for that day. To borrow a metaphor from Neil Gaiman, 'that mountain is far off, but every morning I wake up ready to take a few steps closer to it'."

Seventy

"I live for the moment I can quit this job and become a music teacher. I love teaching music. Everything else is just a compromise of who I am. I have to bide my time and patiently wait until I have accomplished financial independence in order to seriously delve into the low-income world of a music teacher, but I will be oh so happy."

Seventy-One

"I think the real world is pretty shit. The only way to remedy that is to create worlds of my own -- art. It is for this reason that I have decided to become an illustrator."

Seventy-Two

"There is so much wrong with this world. There is so much injustice. There are so many oppressed under regimes, patriarchy, and late-stage capitalism. My passion is international law. I am young and naive, but I have a plan and I need to see it executed."

Seventy-Three

"I live for belly dancing. Been shimmying for 3 years now and in all honesty if I had the means, I'd quit my day job. Dancing is one of the lesser respected jobs out there, but one of the most beautiful in my mind."

Seventy-Four

"I started an opera company with my girlfriend called Kiez Oper, which is German for Neighborhood Opera. The basic point was to take opera away from the stuffy, rich, elitist crowd that seems to hold the monopoly on it at this point in time, and to bring it back to the people! It started off as being an art form for everyone and at the end of the day, it is just another way of telling a story. We put on our first production in July by going into debt and doing it on a shoestring. It was held over two nights in the garden of a techno club in Berlin. For 10 euros, you got a whole opera and a chance to party after in the same place until well into the next day. We barely slept for about two months putting it all together, it was crazy at the time but both nights sold out and I wouldn't change a single thing about it!"

Seventy-Five

"For my hobbies. I love sculpting. Something about shaping clumps of clay into a piece that moves people to tears. Something about creating. Something about using my fingers to express what's felt in my heart."

Seventy-Six

"I want to know about everything. I live for knowledge and understanding, and I am going to die in the pursuit of it."

Seventy-Seven

"I'm a self-proclaimed climate change crusader. I wake up
every morning with the intention of moving this planet one
step closer to long-term habitability. I will do everything in my
power."

Seventy-Eight

"Music. The fact that most of the music I will ever hear in my life probably lies ahead of me is so exciting, especially since I consider my taste to be diverse. I can't wait to discover new things, bask in the nostalgia of older music, pass on my collection to my children, and learn from them what wonders they find in music. I really don't know what my life would be like without music. It is therapeutic, it is everything to me. I've heard songs that make me laugh, make me angry, and songs that make me weep uncontrollably. The idea that there is a connection between every human that can often bypass language barriers just with the mood of a song is what I live for. In a sense, music is an adventure to me."

Seventy-Nine

"I will not stop living until I become a famous author! I don't
know what I'll write about but that's half the fun, never
knowing when inspiration will hit you! I keep on living so that
I can one day write a book that will change people's lives!"

Eighty

"I live for my writing, for the love of writing. Entertaining some folks with a good story and maybe living comfortably enough for the rest of my days would be nice too."

Eighty-One

"Music. I write my own songs, most of which are deeply personal. Whenever life gets me down, I write a song about it and sing until my lungs are sore. No matter what happens in my life I will be able to close my eyes and sing about it and it will always make me feel better, nobody and nothing can take that away from me!"

Eighty-Two

"As a musician, I live to make people dance."

Eighty-Three

"Music. I am never as happy as I am when I'm on stage and there's a huge crowd cheering me on, there's no experience like it. Every time I listen to or play music, I get a huge buzz. I wouldn't be the same person without it."

PART SIX

For Career

Eighty-Four

"This might seem sad to some, but I don't care right now, I live for my work. I work super long hours in a very "corporate" field where the ethos among people my age is that you're supposed to complain about it and say that you hate it but that thank God it pays well. Seriously, it seems like EVERYONE complains, but the truth is, I really like what I do. Sure, I have other things in my life, and I cherish my time to hike, have quiet drinks with friends, play golf, and travel, and whenever I'm in a relationship I do everything I can to make sure that work demands don't interfere, but right now, I get up and go every morning for my super-corporate long-hours job. It's not the "success" so much as it is the job itself."

"I'm in school in New Zealand and my great, grand plan is to move to America to be a film score composer. Currently, all my drive is channeled toward getting me there. I'm currently living for my own future career, really."

Eighty-Six

"Success, and to make sure that the risk my parents took to immigrate and invest in my future does not go to waste."

Eighty-Seven

"Special education. Five years ago, I never would have pictured myself in this line of work, and I was pleasantly surprised at how thoroughly rewarding it is."

Eighty-Eight

"Well... I wasn't sure what I was getting up for the last couple of years. Now I get up every day to go to work and deal with a job that I don't particularly care for... My reason for doing this is this job is just a stepping stone, and I want to see how far I can get in this industry. I'm primed for stepping into a low-level management role. Ultimately, I would like to get into a Regional Manager/Director role, and if I can get into hotel ownership then that would be tops. My drive to succeed in this industry is what pushes me to do the best I can at work every day."

Eighty-Nine

"My work. I'm just starting out in my career as a surgeon, and it is all consuming. Sleep and food are optional on a daily basis, reading and knot tying are not, if you want clinical and technical excellence."

Ninety

"Right now, it is success; not the only reason but it's turning into a passion. I'm going to build a unicorn from the ground up. Maybe even expand into a multinational corporate empire."

Ninety-One

"For the very very slim chance that I transfer into a good university and get through 10 more years of school to achieve my dream of being a scientific researcher. If I didn't have a life goal, I don't know whether I'd have a reason to live."

Ninety-Two

"After being a very shitty student for most of my life, focusing on dating and playing video games, dropping out of one university, and moving back home, I realized that I wanted to be a doctor. Where I'm from–Sweden–you need to have the highest grades or pretty much ace the SATs and such to get into med school, but I pulled my act together and I'm now two years from graduating with my M.D. My reason for getting up in the morning is self-fulfillment and working towards finally becoming a surgeon."

PART SEVEN

For God

Ninety-Three

"Jesus. Devotion to Jesus."

Ninety-Four

"I live for Jesus. I live to show love to others I meet, just as He told us to. It's all about spreading joy in a dark world."

Ninety-Five

"I live for Jesus Christ. According to God, our purpose is to glorify God in the world, and the way that you glorify Him is by serving and loving human beings. By being the image bearers of God on this earth, God intends that we spread love and compassion to others. Jesus said, "I came that they may have life, and have it abundantly." By God providing discernment on how we should live our lives and saying we should live our lives for him, He doesn't mean to be withholding, but rather provide us with a way to be free from the burden of never being good enough. I want to note the difference between the Old Testament and New Testament commandments. The Old Testament commandments are still the word of God, and generally good things, but they were designed for a certain time. The coming of Jesus places us under grace and not under the law. While the law is important, Jesus tells us that the most important thing is to 'Love the Lord your God with all your heart and with all your soul and with all your mind.' This is the first and greatest commandment. And the second is like it: 'Love your neighbor as yourself.' All the Law and the Prophets hang on these two commandments By accepting Jesus as our savior, coming to Him humbly, and admitting when we've done wrong, we are free from constantly trying to be good enough. Since accepting Christ into my life, I feel like I have been more open-handed and kinder to my fellow man, not because I felt an obligation to be, but because my perspective was radically changed. If the most perfect being who ever existed died and suffered for this person, why can't I take the time to be a friend to them, to pour the gifts I've been given back out to others? This isn't to my credit, but to God's. As someone who used to suffer from suicidal bouts of depression and came to Jesus later in life, I can confidently say Jesus has given me something greater to live for, and my life has been more richly blessed.

"Back in the time of the ancient Greeks, there were two schools of philosophy. One of them, as far as I can recall, said that the purpose of life was happiness. The second one said that the purpose of life is love. Which one do I agree with? Well, back in middle school, I lived very naively–I said that all I wanted to do was win. I thought the purpose of life was for me to win and get as much as I can. Afterward, I realized that winning is not any form of permanent satisfaction. As they say at church, don't pursue any worldly needs, for worldly needs and these primitive desires will never be able to satisfy you. Rather, you should pursue heavenly needs. Or satisfaction from respecting the law of God. And once you pursue these divine theological ends, then you will receive the true meaning of life.

So, what do I live for? Do I necessarily live for God? Maybe. I've recently just become religious... Back in Las Vegas, there was a group of Christians preaching and handing out copies of the Bible. And so, I was like, you know what, I've never read the Bible before. I grabbed one, and I read through the whole thing. I thought, 'I'm not sure if I'm necessarily ready to begin believing in all the stories of the Bible, but I am willing to follow this set of ideals.' That's how I wanted to develop into the crux of your question, which is, 'What do you live for?' As Benjamin Franklin said, 'It is better to live well than to live long.' I largely agree. I think that a successful life is probably not one where you focus on happiness nor love, but rather one where you live according to your ideals as best as possible. My ideals are not killing, honesty, and fairness. I'm a man of principle. I would consider my life to be complete if I can live through the whole thing in adherence to my principles, such that once I must answer to God, I will be able to say, 'I lived a full life.' Then, I will have succeeded."

Ninety-Six

"To serve my Lord and Savior Jesus Christ. Unless you have read His teachings and understand who He is, my answer may not make sense to you. I live for Jesus Christ. He is our Creator and he made us for one purpose: to know and love Him for eternity. The highest joy possible for His creatures is to be in a growing relationship with Him. We don't start off life in that relationship; we begin it when we place faith in the words of Christ and His death on our behalf on the cross. We have the intellectual capacity to study the world with science and get a glimpse at His infinite mind. We love our friends and family and experience a glimmer of His unending love. The beauty of God's heart for His people is seen in that, while we were living in ignorance and hostility toward Him, He came to earth as a man and took the penalty we deserved for our rebellion against Him so we could be restored to Him forever."

Ninety-Seven

"For The God of the Christian bible who created the universe and each one of us. The same God who, when we broke His law and rebelled against Him and deserved punishment, paid the penalty by being born a human and died on a cross for us. The same God who conquered death by rising from the dead Easter morning and offered us salvation, resurrection, eternal life, and a relationship with the God who loves us more than we could ever imagine."

PART EIGHT

Ninety-Eight

"I am in the middle of the shittiest time of my life, and I wouldn't trade it for a second. Can't be happy without experiencing pain. I live for life."

Ninety-Nine

"Right this moment, you're alive. But you're not going to live again. Ever. Time will go on. The Earth will be eaten up by the Sun. Stars will be born. And stars will die. Galaxies will collide. Infinite years will pass. You, however, will cease to exist in some 15,000 days. You'll see nothing, hear nothing, feel nothing, ever. Tomorrow you'll have one less day. Start living."

One Hundred

"Sex. Days spent out in nature. Drinking with friends.
Awesome moments in class with my students. Travel. Meeting
new people. Awesome books. Badass movies. The new episode
of Doctor Who. I could go on and on...
I once was talking to a guy who was always complaining about
things he didn't like. I said he should like more stuff and told
him to list 10 things he liked immediately. It took him at least
half an hour to come up with 10 things.
So, he asked me: 'Fine, what do you like?'
We were one mile into a 5-mile hiking trail. I spent the entire
rest of the hike listing things I like. I never run out.
I said: 'Music (both old stuff I love and good new stuff.) The
Daily Show. My houseplant, Frank. My pet snake, Naomi. My
son. His wife, my granddaughter. Flowers in spring. Warm
rain in the summer. Pretty leaves in the fall. Fresh snow in the
winter. Falling in love. Hot chocolate on a cold day. Ice cream
on a warm day. The first beer after mowing the lawn. My
motorcycle. Driving my car too fast. Dive bars. Goth clubs.
Goth women! And while I'm at it, vinyl clothes! Oh, and
corsets. Leather. The smell of new leather.'

And I could keep going, but I wouldn't want to bore you."

One Hundred One

"It's either this or nothing. It's actually quite a good attitude to have, I find, since you tend to think of anything that happens in your life as just another chapter."

"I've always thought that whether people realize it or not, we all live for beauty. If there weren't beautiful things to indulge myself in, I don't think I could go on living."

One Hundred Three

"Dying. I love music, movies, my family, everything about sound, Adventure Time, sleeping, coffee, food, love, interaction with other people, Magic the Gathering, camping, learning, standup comedy, animals, driving with my friends, the list never ends. But I cannot wait to see what happens when I die."

One Hundred Four

"I live for a lot of things. I couldn't say which is the most important, though. I guess I'll have to backtrack a little to explain myself. The first thing I live for is life. As generic as that sounds, it's true. I'm only 24, yet I've had countless friends pass away so far during my time here. Car accidents, suicides, murders, natural causes. All too young; too soon. But there was only one death that rocked me to my core and changed my views on everything. It would be five years ago, this January. One of my mom's oldest friends passed away from a heart attack. I knew him well. He was a terrific human being. She called me one morning, sobbing. At first, I was pissed at her–it was my day off from school. I wanted to sleep in. The anger stopped when I heard her cry. It took her a good five minutes to get the words 'Ron died last night' out of her throat. I sternly told her to not move and that I would be home as soon as I could be. "Home" was almost 200 miles away, as I was attending school on the other side of the state. But I threw clothes in my backpack, put on some shoes, and rushed out the door to the bus station. I was home within three hours. And I never saw my mom so upset.

That moment of pure vulnerability towards life shook me. To a point of no recovery to this day. I still have moments where my heart stops beating, and I lose my breath. Where I feel this rush of sadness wash over me as I realize that one day, I won't be anything. And it's painful. Probably the most painful thing I've ever felt. At first, I had panic attacks. Multiple times a day. In class, in my dorm room, out with friends, in the shower. I couldn't escape that feeling of pure mortality. Since then, I've worked towards living the best life I could. To not take anything for granted because of how lucky we are to be here. To have a shot at whatever this is. To be happy. To laugh, to cry, to smile, to sing, to dance, to love. I question everything and am satisfied by nothing.

It's both the best and worst feeling anyone could have.

So, as I said, I live for life. And the thing I live for most besides that generic and unfathomable thing is the people in my life. Family, friends, strangers, and enemies. I take no one I meet for granted, for they all have the ability to teach me something. To be there for me. A shoulder to cry on or a partner in crime. Work on your relationships. There should be no cause for hatred in your life. Especially towards another human being. We're all here. None of us asked to be. Our time is limited. Make the most of it."

One Hundred Five

"Have fun. Travel the world. Garner as much knowledge as possible. Die."

One Hundred Six

"I live to discover something new in this world. In my opinion, true intelligence comes from discovering rather than understanding. Anyone can absorb and regurgitate information, but looking for new things within our universe and re-writing our definition of reality is my ambition. I just don't know where to start."

One Hundred Seven

"Nobody's last words are, 'I wish I had spent more time at work' or 'I wish I had achieved more career goals.' There's an interesting line to be found, though, between the amount of time one puts towards work and other pursuits. The ideal, of course, is when work does not feel like work. However, not everyone can be Banksy or Jane Goodall. I feel that as long as one is working towards achievements that they care about, they are succeeding in living. If one wants to cure cancer, working in the research department of an immunology and oncology hospital is their calling. They may then have a clear separation between home life and work life, but at the end of the day, they know they're making a difference.

Meanwhile, if you want as many personal experiences as possible, perhaps a job like a truck driver could be fulfilling. You travel a ton, make bank, and have months off at a time to spend however you like. It's not like you're blowing through money in the "on" season.

The hardest part is finding what you want to achieve with your life and overcoming that nagging suspicion that nothing matters, the thought that often leads to nihilism.

Personally, I get too comfortable too fast and then languish. As long as I have projects I am working on and towards, and people to share the fruits of my labor with, I'll feel fulfilled. This comes in the form of:

Learning a new language and showing off my skills to native speakers.

Making art for myself and, mostly, as gifts for friends and family. I'm good at it, I appreciate the praise, and I love that people feel warm inside knowing I put hours of work, creativity, and emotion into something for them.

New experiences. Silent raves, new hikes, new cities, travel. This branches into exposing people to new experiences. Even if I've been to a cave 15 times, it is still awesome to take new people there and show them how to get through the tough parts of it and give them a sense of wonder and achievement. I'm still looking for the underlying passion of my life, as are you, which is why I presume you are writing this book in the first place, but the search is just as fulfilling as the discovery sometimes."

One Hundred Eight

"Had a heart attack 3 weeks ago, now I live because I still fucking can. Before that happened, I was taking the next day for granted."

One Hundred Nine

"Sartre, but only because I read him without understanding."

One Hundred Ten

"I'm just killin' time, man."

One Hundred Eleven

"Life is an adventure. Each day contains new opportunities to explore myself and billions of humans surfacing this Earth! It's a unique adventure that only I get to experience, and that will only happen once. I live to see the sunrise as I listen to birds sing their songs on a foggy spring morning. I live to see the ocean stretch indefinitely beyond my view. I live to chat with my friends about the meaning of our existence and how the weather has been today. Life is what you make it, and I try to make the most of it."

One Hundred Twelve

"Not sure really, but it would be even harder to come up with something to die for. Better to just keep it status quo until I figure the first one out. There isn't something to live for, per se, rather that there doesn't seem much point in dying. I figure with there being so many ways to die that one of them would have gotten me by now, but nope. I live my life day to day basically surprised that I have lasted this long. I get the feeling that if I'm ever involved in a fatal car accident, the moments before impact I will think 'Sheesh, it's about time'."

"I guess the proper question here, from my perspective, would be: What is it that makes you not want to not live? And my answer to that would be quite simple: I am familiar with life. Life is comfortable for me. I know nothing of what it is to be dead. Are you just... nothing? I'm not willing to find out if I can avoid it."

One Hundred Fourteen

"Death is not yet preferable to living another day. No reason to live, no reason to die. Apathy and habitual breathing seem to be the thing keeping me going."

One Hundred Fifteen

"Wake up, eat, work, Instagram while working, come home,
Instagram, eat, TikTok, sleep. Repeat."

One Hundred Sixteen

"I attempted suicide through heroin overdose on the 16th of October in 2011 at 22 years old. Since then, I have lived my life as if each day was a gift I shouldn't have, remaining grateful for each and every beautiful thing I see.

I've realized that the things I saw as weaknesses within myself can become my biggest strengths if I work at removing fear and harnessing them. I buy a coffee for the person behind me in line every day. Most of the time, they just thank me and smile before going on their way.

Some people seem angry, like I have no right to do that and that I'm overstepping some imaginary boundary between strangers. I simply ask them to take the money they would have spent on their coffee and buy someone else's the next day. I live for moments like those, knowing that as small as it may seem, my actions are changing someone else's day tomorrow without me being directly involved.

Live each day like it's your last. For me, that is no longer pumping heroin into my veins and not giving a fuck about anyone else. To me, it means working my ass off to make others happy. I make choices that will decide how people remember me when I die, and between the options of being viewed as the guy who hated the world and never lived up to his potential or the guy who brought out the best in others and found reasons to smile every day, I'll take the latter. This is what I live for."

"I live for my dog. As sappy as it is, he was a stray that my ex-girlfriend found but was never attached to as she was with the dog she already had. The only thing I wanted from the split was to keep the dog, and now I get to see him every morning and treat him like a prince. He always cheers me up when I am down."

One Hundred Eighteen

"My folks. I am the middle child, and I am the only sibling who wanted to stay in the area. I don't think my older/younger brother keeps in touch with them as I would in their situation, so I make sure to see them and call them when given the chance. They deserve it."

One Hundred Nineteen

"My job. Crazy but I enjoy it and more so the people I get to work with. We are tight-knit and practically like family, so it is important I get to see them Mon through Fri between 9-5."

"Well, I am not skilled enough to answer this for myself. But a really wonderful essay I read about this aimlessness is "The Achievement of Desire" by Richard Rodriguez. Truly a marvelous work in which he writes about how his life was so thoroughly based around education he failed to find meaning in it until he finally abandoned his studies. Another would be "The American Scholar" by Ralph Waldo Emerson. Both of these texts are pretty deep and will require that you take some time aside to really ponder the meaning of the authors, but in the end, you'll take away what's important to you. I found these essays to be quite captivating."

One Hundred Twenty-One

"Poetry, science, my woman."

One Hundred Twenty-Two

"The main reason I get out of bed in the morning is coffee. The main reason I stay out of bed is the possibility of more coffee."

One Hundred Twenty-Three

"I live for a lot of reasons, but lately it's been the days where I get to lose myself in a day of climbing and hiking. The views I've seen are both breathtaking and sobering. Really makes you understand how small you are."

One Hundred Twenty-Four

"I live for yesterday. For every day that passes, I gain new
nuggets of information, intriguing facts, and different
perspectives from other people. Each night when I go to sleep,
it gets filed away to bring out later, where you will relive the
memories of the origin of the information, be it the person or
place, you get to relive it. Each day is unique and if you only
look forwards or at the "now" you lose sight of what happened
or your reasons for it. Memories are the only thing that stay
with you forever, possessions will come and go, so will people
in your life, but never will your memories of them disappear.
They might tarnish or fade, but for better or for worse they are
with you forever."

One Hundred Twenty-Five

"A look my wife gives me, the satisfaction of finishing a book, coffee, and a bong hit on Sunday morning. I live for life and the simple things that eventually add up to a great life."

One Hundred Twenty-Six

"To go to sleep a better person than I woke up as."

One Hundred Twenty-Seven

"Nothing, I'm sick of everything frankly."

One Hundred Twenty-Eight

"I'll tell you one thing -- I don't live for "happiness."
Happiness seems like the most ridiculous thing to strive for,
and it baffles me every time someone cites it as a life "goal."
Happiness is fleeting; absolutely no state of mind is
permanent, and living your life to obtain high dopamine levels
seems dishonest and avoidant. I don't know exactly what I'm
living for. Creating order, analyzing, giving meaning to things,
and creating meaning for others. Those sound like the best to
me. We live in chaos, and if we can find significance in the
chaos, either by embracing it or simplifying it, that seems
right. And rewarding."

One Hundred Twenty-Nine

"Walking around and looking at stuff. I seriously could just walk around and check stuff out all day every day. Every city I go to, I avoid transit. I just walk around and explore. I love it."

One Hundred Thirty

"I get up in the morning because I genuinely enjoy being alive and cherish it."

"I'm 17. I live for experience. I live for higher education and for love. I live for the next generation of technology, to see how politics and society change over time. I live for media, I live for my pets and animals I hope to save in my future vet career, I live for friendship."

"I don't really know. I just do what I have to and wait for a real reason to live. I mean it'll come around eventually, won't it?"

"Just living itself. I plan to be forgotten when I'm gone."

One Hundred Thirty-Four

"I don't know why I live. I would assume, mostly because that's what I've always done. And I'm damn too lazy to change my habits."

One Hundred Thirty-Five

"Why I live...? Because why not..?"

"I don't know, nothing in particular. Maybe one day I'll find something worth living for."

One Hundred Thirty-Seven

"The day I can finally find a way of killing myself painlessly."

One Hundred Thirty-Eight

"I live for those who can't. I have many friends that have died in combat. I try to honor them by living my life to the fullest because anything less would be ungrateful of their sacrifice."

One Hundred Thirty-Nine

"Life. It is amazing to be alive and see life around us."

One Hundred Forty

"Friends and volleyball. Not that they are the only reasons.
But holy shit is volleyball fun."

One Hundred Forty-One

"The hope of a better day."

One Hundred Forty-Two

"Mostly I just think that, hey, we're all gonna be dead for most of eternity, no need to rush. Any source of actual satisfaction/happiness is too random to rely on."

"I live to see the beauty and wonder in the world and in myself, and to bring joy to the ones I love. I live to put all my thinking and suffering to good use for myself and others so that we can avoid the same mistakes I've made. And lastly, I live to discover the secrets of existence, such as philosophical, moral, and scientific questions."

One Hundred Forty-Four

"So many things... so I'm just gonna give you a list:
To sing every day, to find someone with whom I can share
everything, to be strong and healthy, to open my own bakery
someday, to become the master of myself in every way through
meditation, to never stop learning, and so much more..."

"I live for the thrill. God, it just fills me with so much electricity. Every time never fails. And it only ever gets better."

One Hundred Forty-Six

"My dad and vinyl records."

"Being content with who I am. I am–and always have been, really–a mess of self-loathing because of what I am. I've been able to shrug off what others say, though it kinda works against me because most people say positive things. All that matters is what I feel, and I hate myself. I am alive now because I want to see if I can be okay with myself, ever. If not, I'm done."

One Hundred Forty-Eight

"For seeing my soon to be wife's smile. To be a tiny bit closer to my hopes for the next few years. There are many more but those are the main ones."

One Hundred Forty-Nine

"Motorcycles and my high school love."

"To study hard in college and work hard to get a well-paying job, so that I can provide for my future family. And also, those mornings off college when I can get up early but chill at home drinking coffee, listening to music, and reading the news. Heaven."

"I get up because I have so much anxiety in the morning. What do I live for? Excellent question. I would have to say it's the dream of raising a family with a reliable job. I have done absolutely nothing in the past 6 years to reach my goal, but dream."

One Hundred Fifty-Two

"I live to see what the day has in store for me, whether it be good or bad. Life may be tough and difficult, but at the same time it's the most beautiful thing in the world."

One Hundred Fifty-Three

"In games, I have trouble picking a certain class and sticking with it. I create alts and want to understand how each class works rather than looking around and enjoying the area. Now, in my life I see myself at an intersection all the time:
The one path is in business, entrepreneurship, and making money. This is because I want to have an apartment high in the sky while looking over a city skyline.
Another path is where I will stay with what I am studying at the moment: I'm currently in year 4 of my bachelor's in cultural heritage. I would be ending up in a museum and living happily.
Another is where I travel a lot.
There are also others but those are minor things, like helping indie musicians and getting people together to make an art festival like Oerol (it's Dutch).
So, you ask me what I live for? I don't know yet, maybe I can mix all of these together and put in a little more family and some significant other and voila, there is my endgame."

One Hundred Fifty-Four

"I haven't watched all the movies yet."

"Because if I kill myself, the people who have fucked me over throughout the years win. And I refuse to give them the satisfaction."

"To prove people who didn't believe in me wrong, and prove that I have a far greater life than what their dreams could possibly imagine."

One Hundred Fifty-Seven

"My mom was a crackhead prostitute, my dad has been in jail since I was 1, I was adopted by abusive grandparents and kicked out at 16. Every day I get out of bed, text my beautiful girlfriend, get in my nice civic, and go to my workplace. I beat the odds. I work in enterprise-level IT as a network analyst, didn't go to college because of money, so while everyone else was out partying after high school and in college I was at home learning anything I could about technology the internet could teach me. I beat the odds every day. I live for beating the odds."

<h1 style="text-align:center">One Hundred Fifty-Eight</h1>

"My brother first. Also, the ability to experience nature and museums and make a difference in either of those subjects. I would like to say love, but I think I've had enough of that."

One Hundred Fifty-Nine

"I have to create something amazing."

One Hundred Sixty

"Climbing, love, and snowboarding. Winter is coming! It's my favorite season. Are you excited?"

One Hundred Sixty-One

"Simply because I want to be alive. I want to be able to do amazing things. I want to fall in love again, I want to form a band, I want to skydive. I just want to be able to do some of the many things that I have the opportunity to do.
I'm probably the laziest person I know but one day I'll get up off my ass and do some of these things and it will be awesome!"

One Hundred Sixty-Two

"Skateboarding. I've been skateboarding every single day since I was 7 years old. I actually cannot fathom what people who don't skateboard do with their free time."

One Hundred Sixty-Three

"There are billions of people out there with really interesting
stories, and I haven't heard them all yet."

One Hundred Sixty-Four

"To prove everyone wrong who ever gave up on me. And to
find the people who won't."

"I live on because I haven't achieved anything yet in my life. I don't want to be just a statistic when I die. I want to be someone that everyone misses."

One Hundred Sixty-Six

"I live because my body hasn't died...that is all."

"I live for the dream that I will, someday, be throwing my leg over a sport bike of my own once again to sweep through the mountain roads of North Georgia."

"Not sure anymore, it's been like this for a while. Maybe that's why I sleep a lot. One day I'll never wake up, that's what I'm truly waiting for."

One Hundred Sixty-Nine

"I'm probably alive right now because I don't want to be a part of another stupid army suicide statistic. Seriously, if more military guys just stopped killing themselves, we probably wouldn't have to watch as many anti-suicide PowerPoints, because they don't do a thing anyway. Somebody in my platoon committed suicide, not one week after our last 4-hour anti-suicide PowerPoint briefing."

One Hundred Seventy

"I wouldn't say there's anything in particular that I live for…I just live, because what else would I do? Die? That'd be silly. I was suicidal as a teenager, but if I'd succeeded then, I wouldn't have met my best friend. I had some suicidal thoughts in college, but if I'd succeeded then, I wouldn't have gotten the chance to work with owls, which is basically the coolest thing ever. I figure that life is so full of surprises that I can never rule out the possibility of good things happening, even when it seems impossible…and I want to be around for as much of it as I can.

Those two things I mentioned—my best friend and the owls—are what I would cite as the things I live for. If life were perfect, I would live with my best friend and spend all of my free time either training owls or doing artwork. As it stands, I smile every time I hear my best friend's voice, and I spend as much time with the owls and my art as I can."

One Hundred Seventy-One

"I live for the quest of finding out why I keep going. Hope I never find out."